INVESTIGATING

EARTH SYSTEMS™

AN INQUIRY EARTH SCIENCE PROGRAM

INVESTIGATING WATER AS A RESOURCE

Michael J. Smith Ph.D.
American Geological Institute

John B. Southard Ph.D.
Massachussetts Institute of Technology

Colin Mably
Curriculum Developer

Developed by the American Geological Institute
Supported by the National Science Foundation and
the American Geological Institute Foundation

IT's ABOUT TIME™

Published by
It's About Time Inc., Armonk, NY

It's About Time, Inc.

84 Business Park Drive, Armonk, NY 10504
Phone (914) 273-2233 Fax (914) 273-2227
Toll Free (888) 698-TIME
www.Its-About-Time.com

Publisher
Laurie Kreindler

Project Editor
Ruta Demery

Creative Artwork
Dennis Falcon

Senior Photo Consultant
Bruce F. Molnia

Design
John Nordland

Safety Reviewer
Dr. Ed Robeck

Photo Research
Caitlin Callahan

Studio Manager
Joan Lee

Production
Burmar Technical Corporation

Associate Editor
Al Mari

Technical Art
Stuart Armstrong

Illustrations and Photos

W3, W22, W23, W25, W26, W28, W34, W35 (bottom), W59, technical art by Burmar Technical Corporation
Wxii, W1, W6, W9, W13, W19, W42, W45, W46, California Department of Water Resources
Wxi (top right), Caitlin Callahan
Wv, Wxii, W4, W10, W17, W27, W33, W36 (top), W39, W44, W50, W54-W55, W61, illustrations by Dennis Falcon
Wxi (bottom right), W5, W12 (bottom), Bruce Molnia
W12 (top), John Nordland
Wxi (top left), W15, W29, W37, W48, W57, PhotoDisc
Wxi (bottom left), W21, Doug Sherman, Geo File Photography
W7, South Florida Water Manangement District
W32, Robert Suter, Vassar College
W16, United States Geological Survey

All student activities in this textbook have been designed to be as safe as possible, and have been reviewed by professionals specifically for that purpose. As well, appropriate warnings concerning potential safety hazards are included where applicable to particular activities. However, responsibility for safety remains with the student, the classroom teacher, the school principals, and the school board.

Investigating Earth Systems™ is a registered trademark of the American Geological Institute. Registered names and trademarks, etc., used in this publication, even without specific indication thereof, are not to be considered unprotected by law.

It's About Time™ is a registered trademark of It's About Time, Inc. Registered names and trademarks, etc., used in this publication, even without specific indication thereof, are not to be considered unprotected by law.

Printed and bound in the United States of America

ISBN #1-58591-077-5

1 2 3 4 5 QC 05 04 03 02 01

This project was supported, in part, by the
National Science Foundation (grant no. 9353035)

Opinions expressed are those of the authors and not necessarily those of the National Science Foundation or the donors of the American Geological Institute Foundation.

W
ii

Investigating Earth Systems

Acknowledgements

Principal Investigator

Michael Smith is Director of Education at the American Geological Institute in Alexandria, Virginia. Dr. Smith worked as an exploration geologist and hydrogeologist. He began his Earth Science teaching career with Shady Side Academy in Pittsburgh, PA in 1988 and most recently taught Earth Science at the Charter School of Wilmington, DE. He earned a doctorate from the University of Pittsburgh's Cognitive Studies in Education Program and joined the faculty of the University of Delaware School of Education in 1995. Dr. Smith received the Outstanding Earth Science Teacher Award for Pennsylvania from the National Association of Geoscience Teachers in 1991, served as Secretary of the National Earth Science Teachers Association, and is a reviewer for Science Education and The Journal of Research in Science Teaching. He worked on the Delaware Teacher Standards, Delaware Science Assessment, National Board of Teacher Certification, and AAAS Project 2061 Curriculum Evaluation programs.

Senior Writer

John Southard received his undergraduate degree from the Massachusetts Institute of Technology in 1960 and his doctorate in geology from Harvard University in 1966. After a National Science Foundation postdoctoral fellowship at the California Institute of Technology, he joined the faculty at the Massachusetts Institute of Technology, where he is currently Professor of Geology. He was awarded the MIT School of Science teaching prize in 1989 and was one of the first cohorts of first MacVicar Fellows at MIT, in recognition of excellence in undergraduate teaching. He has taught numerous undergraduate courses in introductory geology, sedimentary geology, field geology, and environmental Earth Science both at MIT and in Harvard's adult education program. He was editor of the Journal of Sedimentary Petrology from 1992 to 1996, and he continues to do technical editing of scientific books and papers for SEPM, a professional society for sedimentary geology.

Project Director/Curriculum Designer

Colin Mably has been a key curriculum developer for several NSF-supported national curriculum projects. As learning materials designer to the American Geological Institute, he has directed the design and development of the IES curriculum modules and also training workshops for pilot and field-test teachers.

Project Team

Marcus Milling
Executive Director - AGI, VA

Michael Smith
Principal Investigator - Director
of Education - AGI, VA

Colin Mably
Project Director/Curriculum
Designer - Educational
Visions, MD

Fred Finley
Project Evaluator
University of Minnesota, MN

Lynn Lindow
Pilot Test Evaluator
University of Minnesota, MN

Harvey Rosenbaum
Field Test Evaluator
Montgomery School
District, MD

Ann Benbow
Project Advisor - American
Chemical Society, DC

Robert Ridky
Original Project Director
University of Maryland, MD

Chip Groat
Original Principal Investigator
University of Texas
El Paso, TX

Marilyn Suiter
Original Co-principal
Investigator - AGI, VA

William Houston
Project Manager

Eric Shih - Project Assistant

Original and Contributing Authors

Oceans
George Dawson
Florida State University, FL

Joseph F. Donoghue
Florida State University, FL

Ann Benbow
American Chemical Society

Michael Smith
American Geological Institute

Soil
Robert Ridky
University of Maryland, MD

Colin Mably - LaPlata, MD

John Southard
Massachusetts Institute of
Technology, MA

Michael Smith
American Geological Institute

Fossils
Robert Gastaldo
Colby College, ME

Colin Mably - LaPlata, MD

Michael Smith
American Geological Institute

Climate and Weather
Mike Mogil
How the Weather Works, MD

Ann Benbow
American Chemical Society

Michael Smith
American Geological Institute

Energy Resources
Laurie Martin-Vermilyea
American Geological Institute

Michael Smith
American Geological Institute

Dynamic Planet
Michael Smith
American Geological Institute

Rocks and Landforms
Michael Smith
American Geological Institute

Water as a Resource
Ann Benbow
American Chemical Society

Michael Smith
American Geological Institute

Materials and Minerals
Mary Poulton
University of Arizona, AZ

Colin Mably - LaPlata, MD

Michael Smith
American Geological Institute

Advisory Board

Jane Crowder
Middle School Teacher, WA

Kerry Davidson
Louisiana Board of Regents, LA

Joseph D. Exline
Educational Consultant, VA

Louis A. Fernandez
California State University, CA

Frank Watt Ireton
National Earth Science Teachers
Association, DC

LeRoy Lee
Wisconsin Academy of Sciences,
Arts and Letters, WI

Donald W. Lewis
Chevron Corporation, CA

James V. O'Connor (deceased)
University of the District of
Columbia, DC

Roger A. Pielke Sr.
Colorado State University, CO

Dorothy Stout
Cypress College, CA

Lois Veath
Advisory Board Chairperson
Chadron State College, NE

Pilot Test Teachers

Debbie Bambino
Philadelphia, PA

Barbara Barden - Rittman, OH

Louisa Bliss - Bethlehem, NH

Mike Bradshaw - Houston TX

Greta Branch - Reno, NV

Garnetta Chain - Piscataway, NJ

Roy Chambers Portland, OR

Laurie Corbett - Sayre, PA

James Cole - New York, NY

Collette Craig - Reno, NV

Anne Douglas - Houston, TX

Jacqueline Dubin - Roslyn, PA

Jane Evans - Media, PA

Gail Gant - Houston, TX

Joan Gentry - Houston, TX

Pat Gram - Aurora, OH

Robert Haffner - Akron, OH

Joe Hampel - Swarthmore, PA

Wayne Hayes - West Green, GA

Mark Johnson - Reno, NV

Cheryl Joloza - Philadelphia, PA

Jeff Luckey - Houston, TX

Karen Luniewski
Reistertown, MD

Cassie Major - Plainfield, VT

Carol Miller - Houston, TX

Melissa Murray - Reno, NV

Mary-Lou Northrop
North Kingstown, RI

Keith Olive - Ellensburg, WA

Tracey Oliver - Philadelphia, PA

Nicole Pfister - Londonderry, VT

Beth Price - Reno, NV

Joyce Ramig - Houston, TX

Julie Revilla - Woodbridge, VA

Steve Roberts - Meredith, NH

Cheryl Skipworth
Philadelphia, PA

Brent Stenson - Valdosta, GA

Elva Stout - Evans, GA

Regina Toscani
Philadelphia, PA

Bill Waterhouse
North Woodstock, NH

Leonard White
Philadelphia, PA

Paul Williams - Lowerford, VT

Bob Zafran - San Jose, CA

Missi Zender - Twinsburg, OH

Field Test Teachers

Eric Anderson - Carson City, NV

Katie Bauer - Rockport, ME

Kathleen Berdel - Philadelphia, PA

Wanda Blake - Macon, GA

Beverly Bowers
Mannington, WV

Rick Chiera - Monroe Falls, OH

Don Cole - Akron, OH

Patte Cotner - Bossier City, LA

Johnny DeFreese - Haughton, LA

Mary Devine - Astoria, NY

Cheryl Dodes - Queens, NY

Brenda Engstrom - Warwick, RI

Lisa Gioe-Cordi - Brooklyn, NY

Pat Gram - Aurora, OH

Mark Johnson - Reno, NV

Chicory Koren - Kent, OH

Marilyn Krupnick
Philadelphia, PA

Melissa Loftin - Bossier City, LA

Janet Lundy - Reno, NV

Vaughn Martin - Easton, ME

Anita Mathis - Fort Valley, GA

Laurie Newton - Truckee, NV

Debbie O'Gorman - Reno, NV

Joe Parlier - Barnesville, GA

Sunny Posey - Bossier City, LA

Beth Price - Reno, NV

Stan Robinson
Mannington, WV

Mandy Thorne
Mannington, WV

Marti Tomko
Westminster, MD

Jim Trogden - Rittman, OH

Torri Weed - Stonington, ME

Gene Winegart - Shreveport, LA

Dawn Wise - Peru, ME

Paula Wright - Gray, GA

IMPORTANT NOTICE

This work is based upon work supported by the National Science Foundation under Grant No. 9353035 with additional support from the Chevron Corporation. Any opinions, findings, and conclusions or recommendations expressed in this publication are those of the authors and do not necessarily reflect the views of the National Science Foundation or the Chevron Corporation. Any mention of trade names does not imply endorsement from the National Science Foundation or the Chevron Corporation.

Table of Contents

Introducing Water as a Resource   Wxi

Why Is Water an Important Resource?   Wxii

Investigation 1: Use of Water in Your Home   W1
Using Water as a Resource   W5

Investigation 2: Tracing Water in Your School   W9
Water Distribution Systems   W11

Investigation 3: Sources of Water   W15
Watersheds   W18

Investigation 4: Water Movement on the Planet   W21
The Water Cycle   W28

Investigation 5: The Special Properties of Water   W32
The Properties of Water   W37

Investigation 6: The Quality of Your Water Resources   W42
Water Quality   W45

Investigation 7: Cleaning up Water Resources   W48
Treatment of Drinking Water and Wastewater   W51

Investigation 8: Water Conservation Partnership Plan   W57

Reflecting   W63

The Big Picture   W64

Glossary   W65

Using Investigating Earth Systems

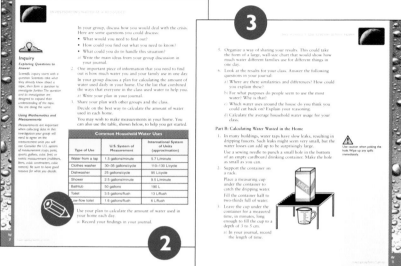

Look for the following features in this module to help you learn about the Earth system.

1. Key Question
Before you begin, you will be asked to think about the key question you will investigate. You do not need to come up with a correct answer. Instead you will be expected to take some time to think about what you already know. You can then share your ideas with your small group and with the class.

2. Investigate
Geoscientists learn about the Earth system by doing investigations. That is exactly what you will be doing. Sometimes you will be given the procedures to follow. Other times you will need to decide what question you want to investigate and what procedure to follow.

3. Inquiry
You will use inquiry processes to investigate and solve problems in an orderly way. Look for these reminders about the processes you are using.

Throughout your investigations you will keep your own journal. Your journal is like one that scientists keep when they investigate a scientific question. You can enter anything you think is important during the investigation. There will also be questions after many of the **Investigate** steps for you to answer and enter in your journal. You will also need to think about how the Earth works as a set of systems. You can write the connections you make after each investigation on your *Earth System Connection* sheet in your journal.

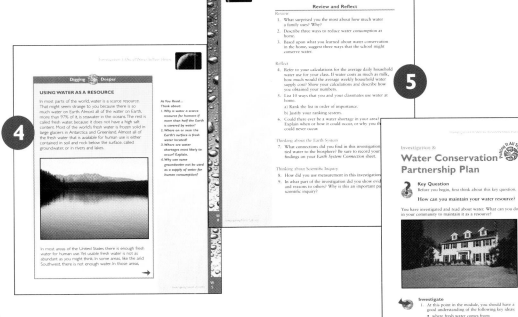

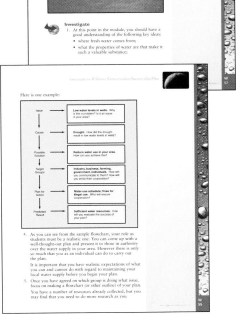

4. Digging Deeper

Scientists build on knowledge that others have discovered through investigation. In this section you can read about the insights scientists have about the question you are investigating. The questions in **As You Read** will help you focus on the information you are looking for.

5. Review and Reflect

After you have completed each investigation, you will be asked to reflect on what you have learned and how it relates to the "big picture" of the Earth system. You will also be asked to think about what scientific inquiry processes you used.

6. Investigation: Putting It All Together

In the last investigation of the module you will have a chance to "put it all together." You will be asked to apply all that you have learned in the previous investigations to solve a practical problem. This module is just the beginning! You continue to learn about the Earth system every time you ask questions and make observations about the world around you.

The Earth System

The Earth System is a set of systems that work together in making the world we know. Four of these important systems are:

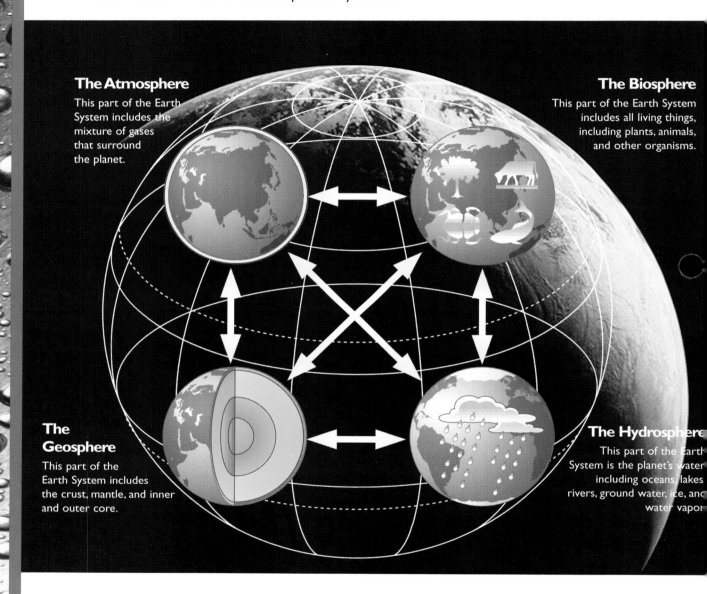

The Atmosphere
This part of the Earth System includes the mixture of gases that surround the planet.

The Biosphere
This part of the Earth System includes all living things, including plants, animals, and other organisms.

The Geosphere
This part of the Earth System includes the crust, mantle, and inner and outer core.

The Hydrosphere
This part of the Earth System is the planet's water, including oceans, lakes, rivers, ground water, ice, and water vapor.

These systems, and others, have been working together since the Earth's beginning about 4.5 billion years ago. They are still working, because the Earth is always changing, even though we cannot always observe these changes. Energy from within and outside the Earth leads to changes in the Earth System. Changes in any one of these systems affects the others. This is why we think of the Earth as made of interrelated systems.

During your investigations, keep the Earth System in mind. At the end of each investigation you will be asked to think about how the things you have discovered fit with the Earth System.

To further understand the Earth System, take a look at THE BIG PICTURE shown on page 64.

Introducing Inquiry Processes

When geologists and other scientists investigate the world, they use a set of inquiry processes. Using these processes is very important. They ensure that the research is valid and reliable. In your investigations, you will use these same processes. In this way, you will become a scientist, doing what scientists do. Understanding inquiry processes will help you to investigate questions and solve problems in an orderly way. You will also use inquiry processes in high school, in college, and in your work.

During this module, you will learn when, and how, to use these inquiry processes. Use the chart below as a reference about the inquiry processes.

Inquiry Processes:	How scientists use these processes
Explore questions to answer by inquiry	Scientists usually form a question to investigate after first looking at what is known about a scientific idea. Sometimes they predict the most likely answer to a question. They base this prediction on what they already know to be true.
Design an investigation	To make sure that the way they test ideas is fair, scientists think very carefully about the design of their investigations. They do this to make sure that the results will be valid and reliable.
Conduct an investigation	After scientists have designed an investigation, they conduct their tests. They observe what happens and record the results. Often, they repeat a test several times to ensure reliable results.
Collect and review data using tools	Scientists collect information (data) from their tests. The data may be numerical (numbers), or verbal (words). To collect and manage data, scientists use tools such as computers, calculators, tables, charts, and graphs.
Use evidence to develop ideas	Evidence is very important for scientists. Just as in a court case, it is proven evidence that counts. Scientists look at the evidence other scientists have collected, as well as the evidence they have collected themselves.
Consider evidence for explanations	Finding strong evidence does not always provide the complete answer to a scientific question. Scientists look for likely explanations by studying patterns and relationships within the evidence.
Seek alternative explanations	Sometimes, the evidence available is not clear or can be interpreted in other ways. If this is so, scientists look for different ways of explaining the evidence. This may lead to a new idea or question to investigate.
Show evidence & reasons to others	Scientists communicate their findings to other scientists to see if they agree. Other scientists may then try to repeat the investigation to validate the results.
Use mathematics for science inquiry	Scientists use mathematics in their investigations. Accurate measurement, with suitable units is very important for both collecting and analyzing data. Data often consist of numbers and calculations.

Introducing Water as a Resource

Did you ever drink water from a well?

Have you ever seen a stream trickling from the side of a mountain?

Have you ever wondered what happens to water after you have used it?

Have you ever thought about how water enters the atmosphere?

Why is Water an Important Resource?

Water is such an important part of your everyday life that it is easy to take it for granted. Getting a drink of water is as simple as turning on the tap. However, this is not the case everywhere. Safe drinking water may be scarce in arid regions or because of drought, floods, and other natural disasters. Of course, water is used for more than drinking, but other uses of water may not be so obvious. You may be surprised to learn that wastewater treatment requires water. Farming, raising livestock, manufacturing, mining, power generation: all of these processes require water.

If you look at a world map, you will see that much of the Earth is covered with water. It would seem as though there should be an endless supply. However, most of this water is in the oceans and is not suitable for human use. The water that you rely on for drinking and other uses comes from rivers, lakes, streams, and below the ground. Evaporation and precipitation replenish this supply in a process called the water cycle.

What Will You Investigate?

You will discover how water as a resource is part of the Earth System.

Here are some of the things that you will investigate:

- how water is used;
- where your water supply comes from;
- how water moves through the Earth System;
- properties of water;
- water management.

You will need to practice your problem-solving skills and be good observers and recorders as you work together with other members of your class.

In the last investigation you will have an opportunity to apply all that you have learned about water resources. You will develop a plan to monitor and conserve the water supply in your community.

Investigation 1:

Use of Water in Your Home

Key Question

Before you begin, first think about this key question.

How is water used in your home?

Think about all the ways that you and your family use water. How do you use water at home every day? Record your thoughts in your journal.

Share your thinking with others in your small group and in your class. Make a list that combines the ways that everyone in the class uses water in their homes.

Materials Needed

For this investigation your group will need:

- empty 2-L cardboard drinking container
- very small sewing needle
- metal rack
- measuring cup or graduated cylinder
- stopwatch or watch with a second hand
- calculator

Investigate

Part A: Estimating Home Water Use

1. Imagine hearing an announcement on the radio that a water shortage in your area has reached a crisis. There are plans to ration the amount of water that each household can use. You have to reduce your water consumption drastically.

Inquiry

Exploring Questions to Answer

Scientific inquiry starts with a question. Scientists take what they already know about a topic, then form a question to investigate further. The question and its investigation are designed to expand their understanding of the topic. You are doing the same.

Using Mathematics and Measurements

Measurements are important when collecting data. In this investigation your group will need to agree on the measurement units you will use. Consider the U.S. system of measurement (cups, pints, quarts, gallons, cubic feet) or metric measurement (milliliters, liters, cubic centimeters, cubic meters). Be sure to have good reasons for what you decide.

In your group, discuss how you would deal with the crisis. Here are some questions you could discuss:

- What would you need to find out?
- How could you find out what you need to know?
- What could you do to handle this situation?

a) Write the main ideas from your group discussion in your journal.

2. One important piece of information that you need to find out is how much water you and your family use in one day.

In your group discuss a plan for calculating the amount of water used daily in your home. Use the list that combined the ways that everyone in the class used water to help you.

a) Write your plan in your journal.

3. Share your plan with other groups and the class.

Decide on the best way to calculate the amount of water used in each home.

You may wish to make measurements in your home. You can also use the table, shown below, to help you get started.

Common Household Water Uses		
Type of Use	**U.S. System of Measurement**	**International System of Units (approximation)**
Water from a tap	1.5 gallons/minute	5.7 L/minute
Clothes washer	30–35 gallons/cycle	110–130 L/cycle
Dishwasher	25 gallons/cycle	95 L/cycle
Shower	2.5 gallons/minute	9.5 L/minute
Bathtub	50 gallons	190 L
Toilet	3.5 gallons/flush	13 L/flush
Low-flow toilet	1.6 gallons/flush	6 L/flush

4. Use your plan to calculate the amount of water used in your home each day.

a) Record your findings in your journal.

5. Organize a way of sharing your results. This could take the form of a large, wall-size chart that would show how much water different families use for different things in one day.

6. Look at the results for your class. Answer the following questions in your journal:

   a) Where are there similarities and differences? How could you explain these?

   b) For what purposes do people seem to use the most water? Why is that?

   c) Which water uses around the house do you think you could cut back on? Explain your reasoning.

   d) Calculate the average household water usage for your class.

Part B: Calculating Water Wasted in the Home

1. In many buildings, water taps have slow leaks, resulting in dripping faucets. Such leaks might seem very small, but the water losses can add up to be surprisingly large.

   Use a sewing needle to punch a small hole in the bottom of an empty cardboard drinking container. Make the hole as small as you can.

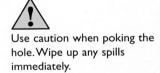

Use caution when poking the hole. Wipe up any spills immediately.

2. Support the container on a rack.

   Place a measuring cup under the container to catch the dripping water.

   Fill the container half to two-thirds full of water.

3. Leave the cup under the container for a measured time, in minutes, long enough to fill the cup to a depth of 3 to 5 cm.

   a) In your journal, record the length of time.

4. Measure the volume of water caught in the cup. Make sure that the cup is resting on a flat surface when you make the measurement. Your sight line should be at the same height as the water level in the cup.

   Estimate the volume to the nearest milliliter.

   a) Record this measurement.

5. Calculate the rate of water loss (volume per unit time) in milliliters per minute.

   Write this measurement in liters per day.

   a) Show your calculations, conversion, and your results in your journal.

6. As a class, compare the values obtained by all of the groups.

   a) Why might the results vary from group to group?

7. In your group discuss how to deal with the water shortage described in Part A. Assume that it is a temporary shortage but that it will last at least a week. Try to be as creative as you can in your approach to the problem.

   Write a commercial to educate and inform citizens about the local water shortage and to explain your proposed solution.

   a) Record your commercial in your journal.

8. Present your commercial to the class.

USING WATER AS A RESOURCE

In most parts of the world, water is a scarce resource. That might seem strange to you because there is so much water on Earth. Almost all of the water on Earth, more than 97% of it, is seawater in the oceans. The rest is called fresh water, because it does not have a high salt content. Most of the world's fresh water is frozen solid in large glaciers in Antarctica and Greenland. Almost all of the fresh water that is available for human use is either contained in soil and rock below the surface, called groundwater, or in rivers and lakes.

In most areas of the United States there is enough fresh water for human use. Yet usable fresh water is not as abundant as you might think. In some areas, like the arid Southwest, there is not enough water. In those areas,

As You Read...
Think about:
1. Why is water a scarce resource for humans if more than half the Earth is covered by water?
2. Where on or near the Earth's surface is fresh water located?
3. Where are water shortages most likely to occur? Explain.
4. Why can some groundwater not be used as a supply of water for human consumption?

water has to be transported long distances from other places in human-made channels called aqueducts. Even in areas with plenty of fresh water there are sometimes

An aqueduct in California.

shortages. Rainfall is the only way that water supplies are replenished. During times of drought, when rainfall is below average for several weeks, months, and even a number of years, water supplies can become dangerously low. Even when rainfall is adequate, water from rivers and lakes might be unusable because of pollution. In some areas, groundwater cannot be used because when it is removed from the ground, nearby wetlands would be damaged by drying up. As the population of the United States continues to grow in the future, water shortages will become more common, because the supply of available water remains the same. Water conservation will become more and more important as time goes on.

Your investigation of the amounts of water used and possibly wasted in your home for these purposes might have surprised you. Most people do not think much

about how much water they use. Perhaps this is partly because you don't pay for it each time you use it, except when you buy bottled water.

There are many ways to conserve water in your home. Some are easier than others. Leaky faucets and leaky toilets waste very large amounts of water, because even though the flow rates are small, they leak all the time. New designs of toilets and washing machines use much less water than older designs, but replacement is expensive. Water-saving shower heads save a lot of water, and they are relatively easy and inexpensive to replace. The most effective ways to reduce water use, however, might be the most difficult. Taking "navy showers" (turning off the water while you're soaping yourself), not planting lavish lawns in areas that are normally arid, and driving an unwashed car are examples of effective and simple ways to conserve water.

Landscaping with plants that require little water can conserve water.

Review and Reflect

Review

1. What surprised you the most about how much water a family uses? Why?

2. Describe three ways to reduce water consumption at home.

3. Based upon what you learned about water conservation in the home, suggest three ways that the school might conserve water.

Reflect

4. Refer to your calculations for the average daily household water use for your class. If water costs as much as milk, how much would the average weekly household water supply cost? Show your calculations and describe how you obtained your numbers.

5. List 10 ways that you and your classmates use water at home.

   a) Rank the list in order of importance.

   b) Justify your ranking system.

6. Could there ever be a water shortage in your area? Explain when or how it could occur, or why you think it could never occur.

Thinking about the Earth System

7. What connections did you find in this investigation that tied water to the biosphere? Be sure to record your findings on your *Earth System Connection* sheet.

Thinking about Scientific Inquiry

8. How did you use measurement in this investigation?

9. In what part of the investigation did you show evidence and reasons to others? Why is this an important part of scientific inquiry?

Investigation 2:

Tracing Water in Your School

Key Question

Before you begin, first think about this key question.

From where does the water supply in your school come, and where does it go?

You have investigated how you and your classmates use water in your homes. Think about how water is used in your school. From where does the water you use come? Where and how does it leave your school when everyone is done with it?

Record your thoughts in your journal. Share your ideas with others in your small group and in your class.

Materials Needed

For this investigation, your group will need to decide what materials you will require.

Investigate

1. In your group think about the following:
   - How and where does water get into your school?
   - Where does water go once it enters the school?

Inquiry

Dividing Tasks

This investigation provides you with an opportunity to mirror the teamwork that often happens in scientific studies. Different groups often take on responsibility for different parts of the study.

Do not enter maintenance areas of the school without permission and adult supervision.

- How much water is used in your school, and how is it used?
- How and where does the water leave the building after it has been used?
- Where does the water go after it has left your school?

Discuss ways you could find out this information.

a) Record the key points of your discussion in your journal.

2. Devise a plan to find out answers to these questions. Things to consider while designing your plan include:

- How will responsibilities be divided among groups and within your own group?
- How will you gather and record the information?
- How will your group present its findings to the rest of the class?

Once you have agreed on a method that will help answer the questions, share it with others in your class.

As a class, develop a plan to find the answers.

a) In your journal record the plan developed by the class.

3. Carry out your plan.

4. When you have found the answers to your questions, present them to your classmates.

   Listen carefully to what others in your class have to say.

   a) In your journal record the information from each presentation that helps you answer the questions.

5. Review your notes from the presentations. Using your notes, answer the following questions:

   a) How many different places does water enter the school?

   b) How is the use of water in your school different from the use of water in your home? How is it the same?

   c) Where does wastewater leave the school?

   d) Where does wastewater go after it leaves the school?

   e) What new questions could you ask about your school's water supply?

Inquiry

Learning from Others

Because different groups may have concentrated on different aspects of the school's water supply, you need to ensure that everyone fully understands the whole picture. You have a responsibility to present your findings to others.

Digging   Deeper

WATER DISTRIBUTION SYSTEMS

In rural areas, most homes and businesses get their water from groundwater. Long ago, wells had to be dug by hand and reached only shallow groundwater. Now, wells can be drilled by machinery to as deep as several hundred feet. In urban and suburban areas, most water is piped in from a central water supply. The water supply might be a river, a natural lake, a reservoir behind a dam, or a number of deep wells. In many big cities, reservoirs are located far away, and the water is brought to the city through aqueducts.

If you have ever tried to stop the flow of water from a hose or pipe with your thumb, or if you have seen a hose or a pipe burst, you know that water pressure is very high. The high pressure ensures that the flow of water is adequate wherever and whenever it is needed.

As You Read...
Think about:

1. What is the main source of water in rural areas?

2. What is the role of pressure in ensuring a supply of water for homes and schools?

3. How is water supplied to homes and businesses in larger towns and cities?

Storing water at a high elevation in a lake or reservoir can produce pressure. Where water is pumped from the ground it is stored in special tanks on hilltops. In home water systems pumps produce the pressure needed.

In urban and suburban areas, water is distributed from the source through large underground pipes, called water mains, under the streets. A map of the water mains in your town would look something like the pattern of branches on a tree or the pattern of tributaries in a

river system. The water mains keep branching out into smaller and smaller pipes until they reach a home or other building, where they enter the building and pass through a water meter. In areas with cold winters, the mains and pipes have to be buried as deep as several feet below the surface to keep them from freezing.

Most of the water that is used inside your home or school remains liquid. It flows through drainpipes into a municipal sewer system or into a septic system connected to the building. A septic system consists of a large tank buried in the ground. The solids in the sewage are slowly digested by microorganisms and converted to sludge. The sludge settles to the bottom of the tank and is pumped out occasionally by special trucks. The wastewater flows out of the tank and into underground pipes that leak water into the ground over a large area.

Municipal sewer systems are the opposite of municipal water systems: they collect the used water and carry it through a network of underground sewer pipes to a central treatment plant. Sewage treatment plants differ in how much they treat the sewage. Some do nothing more than filter out the solid materials. Others treat the sewage in several stages and end up with water that is pure enough to drink! The treated sewage is usually returned to rivers, lakes, or the ocean, or is spread on the ground to soak in. In some places untreated sewage, called "raw sewage," is still dumped directly into rivers, lakes, or the ocean.

Some of the water that is used in your home and school evaporates. Most of the evaporation happens when water is spread over a large area, as in cleaning floors or pavement, or in watering a lawn or garden.

Review and Reflect

Review

1. Look again at the key question for this investigation. What did you learn about your school's water system?

2. What surprised you the most about how water is used in your school? Explain.

3. Draw a diagram showing how water is supplied to your school, and where it goes when it has been used. Label the diagram to show the flow of water.

4. What surprised you the most about how water is supplied or removed from your school? Explain.

Reflect

5. Do you think trends of water use would be the same in a school in another town? In another country? Explain.

6. What do you think your school could do to reduce its water usage?

Thinking about the Earth System

7. How does your school's water supply depend on the hydrosphere?

8. How does your school's water supply depend on the atmosphere?

Thinking about Scientific Inquiry

9. How did you use mathematics as a tool for inquiry?

10. What did you do to present findings in a form that others could see and understand?

Investigation 3:

Sources of Water

Key Question

Before you begin, first think about this key question.

Where does your water come from?

You have seen where water is used, both at home and at school. You have also looked at where it enters and exits the school. Imagine you are a drop of water in a tap at your school. What journey did you have to make to get where you are today?

Write your ideas in the form of a first-person story. For example: "I started my journey as a tiny drop many…" Share your stories with your small group and the rest of the class.

Materials Needed

For this investigation your group will need:

• topographic map of your local area

• map showing industrial sites, waste dumps, etc.

• colored pencils or transparency markers

Investigate

1. Look at a topographic map of your local area.

   Lay a piece of tracing paper or a clear piece of plastic over the map, or obtain a copy of the map.

   a) Using a blue pencil or marker, carefully trace all of the major streams and bodies of water in your community. This is your local stream network.

b) Draw arrows with one of your colored pencils, showing the direction in which the water flows.

c) Lightly shade over the land area drained by your local stream network. This is called your watershed.

Inquiry

Using Maps as Scientific Tools

Scientists collect and review data using tools. You may think of tools as only physical objects such as measuring cups. However, forms in which information is gathered, stored, and presented are also tools for scientists. In this investigation you are using a topographic map as a scientific tool. A topographic map shows the hills and valleys with contour lines. A contour line connects places at the same elevation. Elevations are labeled, usually in feet or meters above sea level.

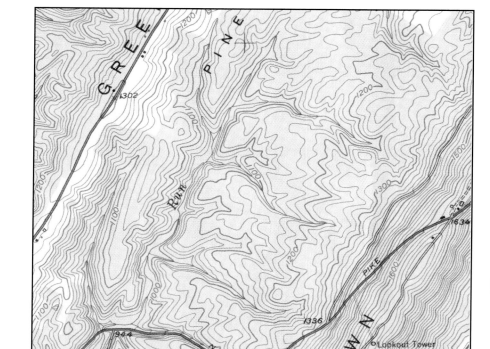

Scale 1:24,000 Contour interval: 20 ft.

2. Locate each of the following on your map:
   - water treatment and wastewater treatment facilities,
   - industrial sites,
   - farms,
   - waste sites and landfills,
   - new, large communities,
   - mines or excavations,
   - recreational areas.
   - any other places that you think might affect the local water supply.

   a) Draw and label each on your map.

3. Use your map to answer the following questions:

   a) Through which areas does the water flow?

   b) What does the water encounter along the way?

   c) Where and how could pollutants enter the watershed?

4. In your group, think of questions about your local water sources that you want to try to investigate.

   Post your questions to share with the class.

   a) Write down other groups' questions and compile a master list.

5. Choose questions for your group to investigate. Think about who you would consult to find answers to your questions.

   a) In your journal write down the question that your group will be investigating.

   b) Write down the answers that you find. Be sure to include the source of your information.

Inquiry

Representing Information

Communicating findings to other scientists is very important in scientific inquiry. In this investigation it is important for you to find good ways of showing what you learned to others in your class. Be sure your maps and diagrams are clearly labeled and well organized.

As You Read...
Think about:

1. **How does gravity control the flow of water?**

2. **What is the main source of water supply for humans?**

3. **What is a watershed?**

4. **What are possible sources of pollution in a watershed?**

6. When everyone has their information, decide on a method of sharing it with others. You might consider making up a "class magazine," in which each group submits an illustrated article about their research (possibly with maps and diagrams).

Digging Deeper

WATERSHEDS

Everybody knows that water flows downhill. The reason is that the force of gravity pulls everything downward toward the center of the Earth. Groundwater also flows from high areas to low areas, but its motion is much more difficult to observe. Water in the pipes in your home can flow upward as well as downward, because the high pressure in the pipes is much greater than the force of gravity.

The source of almost all of the water supplies for human civilization is rainfall or melted snowfall. When rain falls on the land, it either runs off into streams and rivers or it soaks into the ground to become groundwater. The groundwater flows slowly underground and eventually comes back out to the surface at the beds of lakes and rivers.

Every stream or river drains a particular area of the land surface. The land area that is drained by a given river is called the watershed of that river. Watersheds are also called drainage basins. The imaginary line on the land surface that separates the watershed of one river from the watershed of another river is called a divide. Divides follow along the crests of hills and ridges. You can stand on a divide and pour a glass of water from one hand into one watershed and a glass of water from the other hand into another watershed! There are watersheds for groundwater as well as for surface water. Divides between groundwater drainage basins are usually in about the same place as divides between river drainage basins.

Most towns and cities get their water from their own watershed. In some places, especially in large cities, the demand for water is greater than the supply in the local watershed. Then water has to be transported from distant watersheds.

Many substances that are hazardous to human health can enter water supplies. Chemical waste from factories is sometimes dumped into rivers and lakes, or directly into the ground. Pesticides (chemicals that kill insects) applied to farmland enter surface water and groundwater, often in large quantities. Leaks from underground storage tanks for liquids like gasoline go directly into groundwater. Salt put on icy roads in winter pollutes water also, although it is not as hazardous to human health.

Once a pollutant enters a water supply, it is difficult to get rid of it. Some pollutants slowly break down into harmless chemicals. Once the input of pollution is stopped, the pollutant gradually travels downstream and is replaced by unpolluted water. The problem is that it usually takes a long time for pollution to clear up in that way.

As the pollutant travels downstream it is diluted by the addition of water. This causes the concentration of the pollutant to decrease. Often, the concentration becomes low enough for the water to be judged safe for use, but the pollutant is still there.

Review and Reflect

Review

1. Describe the watershed in which you live.
2. Where does your local water come from?
3. Where is your local water treatment facility?

Reflect

4. How does the direction of water flow help you to understand what can get into the watershed?

Thinking about the Earth System

5. On your *Earth System Connection* sheet, write any connections that you have made between water as a resource and the Earth system.

Thinking about Scientific Inquiry

6. How did you use a question as a starting point for inquiry?
7. How did you use tools to collect data?
8. How did you use evidence to develop ideas?
9. Provide at least one new question about water resources that your investigation has raised.

Investigation 4:

Water Movement on the Planet

Key Question
Before you begin, first think about this key question.

How is water recycled in nature?

You have seen where your local water supply comes from. How else does water move through your community? Discuss your ideas with your classmates.

Materials Needed

For this investigation the materials your group will need are listed with each part of the investigation.

Investigate

Part A: Visualizing Water in the Environment

1. Draw a picture of a cloud with rain falling from it, mountains, a stream coming from a mountain, and a body of water. Use the diagram on the following page as an example.

2. Think about places in the picture that water would be in one of its three forms: solid (ice), liquid, or gas (vapor).

    a) Label these places on your diagram.

3. Share your labeled drawings with your group members and then with your class.

    Discuss any differences in the ways you have labeled your drawings.

    a) What evidence do you and your classmates have for your ideas?

    b) What changes might you make to your diagram, based on your discussion?

4. Imagine you are a drop of water.

    a) Describe how you would move throughout the environment pictured in your sketch.

    b) What forces cause you to move?

Part B: Modeling Water in the Environment.
I Flow of Groundwater

1. Set up the materials as shown in the diagram to model the flow of groundwater through gravel, coarse sand, fine sand, and a mixture of all three. Before you begin, develop a hypothesis about the rate of flow through sediments of different sizes.

   a) Record your hypothesis in your notebook. Be sure that your hypothesis includes a prediction and a reason for your prediction.

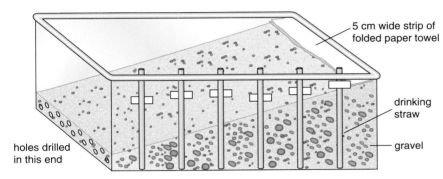

5 cm wide strip of folded paper towel

drinking straw

gravel

holes drilled in this end

2. Suppose you were to spray water onto the paper towel long enough for water to completely soak the gravel so that water flows out the base. Predict the level of water in each of the wells.

   a) On a copy of the experimental setup, indicate the water level you predict in each well. Explain your prediction.

3. With a watering can or spray hose, spray water onto the paper towel. Move the spray back and forth across the paper towel to water the whole width of the box equally.

   Keep on spraying until water flows out from the lower end of the wedge of gravel.

4. Continue to spray.

   Measure the heights of the water levels in each of the straws or tubes through the side wall of the container with the ruler.

   a) Record your measurements.

Materials Needed

For this part of the investigation your group will need:

- clear plastic box (about 40 cm x 20 cm, and at least 15 cm deep)
- package of transparent plastic drinking straws, or six 15 cm lengths of transparent plastic tubing, 6 mm to 12 mm in diameter
- tape
- centimeter ruler
- 2.5 kg aquarium gravel
- paper towel
- watering can or kitchen spray hose
- food coloring
- plastic sheeting
- 2.5 kg coarse sand
- 2.5 kg fine sand

Wear safety goggles. Be sure water draining from the plastic box will be caught by the sink or large container. Wipe up spills immediately.

Inquiry

Modeling

To investigate the flow of groundwater in the environment, you have set up a model. Models are very useful scientific tools. Scientists use models to simulate real-world events and processes. They do this when it is difficult to study the real thing in a controlled way. It is important that you try to model what happens in the real world as accurately as possible.

Using Mathematics

Mathematics is a key tool for scientists. Accurate measurement with suitable units is very important for collecting and analyzing data. In this investigation you must measure time. You also are measuring length. You need to decide on the best unit of length measurement to use.

Dispose of the straws or mark them as contaminated.

5. While spraying, note the time, and put four drops of food coloring in the middle of the paper towel. Continue spraying.

   Watch for colored water to emerge from the lower end of the wedge of gravel.

   a) Record the time when you first see the colored water, and record the later time when the water again becomes clear of coloring.

6. Stop spraying and note the time.

   a) Record this time and then record the later time when the flow of water out the open end of the container has slowed down to a trickle.

7. Remove the gravel and clean up the setup.

   Spread the gravel out on a plastic sheet to allow excess water to drain away.

8. Repeat Steps 2 through 7 with the coarse sand and then with the fine sand in the container.

   a) Record all your observations and data.

9. Repeat Steps 2 through 7 with the mixed material in the container.

   a) Record all your observations and data.

10. Use your results from all parts of the investigation (gravel, coarse sand, fine sand, mixed materials) to answer the following questions:

    a) Describe the pattern of water heights in the tubes you observed. How did it compare to your predictions? How can you account for the pattern you observed?

    b) In which part of the investigation (gravel, coarse sand, fine sand, or mixed material) were the water levels in the straws or tubes the highest? In which part were the water levels the lowest? Why?

    c) In which part of the investigation did it take longest for the water flow to stop after you stopped spraying? Why?

    d) In which part of the investigation did the colored water reach the open end of the container the soonest? In which part did the colored water reach the open end of the container the slowest? Why?

e) How can you explain why there was a nonzero period of time between when you first saw the colored water flow from the open end of the container and when you saw the water become clear again?

II Distillation

1. Set up the equipment for modeling distillation as shown in the diagram.

   Equipment used for distillation is called a still. Since you will be using sunlight as a source of energy, your setup is called a solar still.

   a) Write a prediction of what you think will happen inside the still when you place it in sunlight. Give the reasons for your prediction.

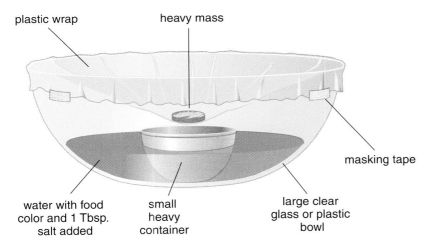

plastic wrap   heavy mass

masking tape

water with food color and 1 Tbsp. salt added   small heavy container   large clear glass or plastic bowl

2. Place the still where it will receive direct sunlight, or under a sun lamp.

   Leave the still in the light for a few hours.

   a) Record your observations.

3. When about a teaspoon of water has collected in the small container, open up the still and remove the small container.

4. Observe the color of the water in the container.

   Your teacher will arrange a taste test of the water.

   a) Record your observations in your journal. How do your predictions compare with what you observed? Explain any differences.

Materials Needed

For this part of the investigation your group will need:

- small but heavy container, like a small drinking glass or coffee mug
- large clear plastic or glass bowl
- water
- food coloring
- tablespoon of salt
- clear plastic wrap
- masking tape
- heavy mass such as a coin
- sun lamp, or a place where there is direct sunlight for at least a few hours

⚠️

Be sure all materials are clean prior to use. Do not use beakers or other scientific equipment for either the bowl or the small container. Be sure that the bowl is placed in a safe location where it will not be broken. Follow the teacher's instructions with respect to the taste test.

Inquiry
Using Evidence

Evidence is very important for scientists. They use evidence that other scientists have collected, as well as evidence they collect themselves.

b) Distillation is the process of making pure water by evaporating impure water and then condensing the water vapor. What evidence do you have distillation occurred?

III Transpiration

Materials Needed

For this part of the investigation your group will need:

- vigorous, leafy plant grown in a pot with bottom drain holes

- water source

- balance or scale

- plastic wrap

- string

- warm, bright area

1. Obtain a potted plant that needs watering.

   Water the plant until excess water runs out of the bottom of the pot.

   Wait until all of the excess water has drained.

2. Wrap the pot tightly in plastic wrap. Be sure to cover the entire soil surface.

   Fit the plastic wrap snugly around the stem of the plant.

3. Find the mass of the potted plant on a balance or scale.

   a) Record the mass of the potted plant in your journal.

   b) Write a prediction of what you think will happen to the mass of the potted plant over the next few days. Give the reasons for your prediction.

   Let the pot sit in a warm, bright area of the classroom for at least one day.

4. Find the mass of the potted plant again.

   a) Record the mass in your journal.

   b) Calculate the decrease in the mass of the potted plant.

   c) Explain any difference that you find in the mass of the potted plant.

Part C: Analyze and Present your Findings

1. In your group, discuss how the drawing you created in Part A could be changed to reflect any new information you discovered in this investigation.

   a) What forces drive water movement?

   b) Where else is water located?

2. As a group, decide on a means to show the rest of the class your findings.

   Present your findings.

   Consider using a chart, a report, a revised drawing, a poster, or a model.

   Revise your findings based on feedback for your classmates.

As You Read...
Think about:

1. How does water change from one form to another on Earth?

2. Where is water stored near the surface of the Earth?

3. What does an example of a "loop" in the water cycle involve?

4. What properties of Earth materials affect the flow of groundwater?

5. Why does groundwater flow so much more slowly than water in a river?

6. What conditions make groundwater a nonrenewable resource?

Digging Deeper

THE WATER CYCLE

Water exists at the Earth's surface as liquid, solid, and vapor. It is forever changing from one of those three states to another. You can easily observe how water changes from liquid to solid by freezing and from solid to liquid by melting. Water also changes from liquid to vapor by evaporation and from vapor to liquid by condensation. Condensation is how clouds and raindrops form. Water can even change from vapor directly into solid; by the process of sublimation. That is how snowflakes are formed, high in the atmosphere.

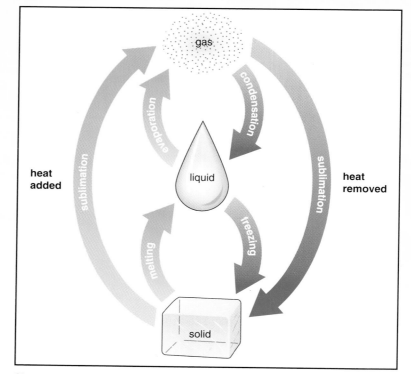

Change of state of water.

The total amount of water near the surface of the Earth stays almost the same through time, but water is always moving from place to place. You can think of places

where water resides, like the ocean or lakes or glaciers, as "reservoirs." Water moves from reservoir to reservoir in various ways. It can move in the form of liquid, solid, or vapor. This complicated movement of the Earth's water is called the water cycle.

One of the most important "loops" in the water cycle involves evaporation of water from the ocean surface, transport in the form of water vapor to the continents by winds, and precipitation as rain or snow on the continents. The rainfall then runs off by way of streams, rivers, and groundwater back to the ocean. You modeled a similar loop with your distillation setup. Another important "loop" in the water cycle involves condensation of water vapor in the atmosphere to form rain, soaking of the rain into the ground, uptake of the water by plant roots, and return of that water, in the form of water vapor, back into the atmosphere by transpiration through the leaves of the plants. You modeled transpiration using a potted plant in this investigation. There are many other "loops" as well. The Earth's water cycle is very complicated in its details.

Groundwater Flow

Most of the materials beneath the Earth's surface are porous. That means that they contain tiny open spaces as well as solids, just like a sponge. The porosity of a material is the percentage of open pore space it contains. Loosely packed sand and gravel can have porosities as high as 25%. Solid rock is much less porous. Many rocks have a porosity of only a small fraction of a percent.

Another important property of Earth materials is their permeability. The permeability describes how easy it is to force a fluid to flow through the pore spaces of the material. Loose sand and gravel have high permeability. Solid rock usually has low permeability. The best sources of groundwater, called aquifers, have high porosity and also high permeability. Sand, gravel, and fractured rock make the best aquifers.

Groundwater flow is much slower than flow in streams and rivers. That is because the passageways through the pore spaces are very small, so there is a lot of friction with the solid walls of the pores. Speeds of flow in streams and rivers are often greater than a meter per second. Groundwater flow is often as slow as several meters per day.

For a large town or city to obtain its water from groundwater, there needs to be a large aquifer. Several widely spaced wells are used to pump water from the aquifer, all at the same time. If the groundwater is replaced as fast as it is pumped, then it is a renewable resource. If the groundwater is pumped faster than it is replaced, however, then the level of the groundwater falls. It becomes more and more difficult to obtain the required water. Then the groundwater is not really a renewable resource, because the replacement might take far longer than a human lifetime!

Review and Reflect

Review

1. How does the size of particles in a material affect the movement of groundwater through the material?

2. How might your model of distillation be used as a source of fresh water?

Reflect

3. Choose one of the processes that you modeled in this investigation. Explain how you could improve the investigation so that your observations could be more easily repeated by others.

4. Describe the movement of water through a "loop" of the water cycle.

Thinking about the Earth System

5. What new connections between water and the biosphere did you notice in the investigation of transpiration?

6. What new connections between water and the atmosphere did you notice in this investigation?

7. What new connections between water and the geosphere did you notice in this investigation?

Thinking about Scientific Inquiry

8. Why are predictions helpful in scientific inquiry?

9. Describe how your examination of evidence is similar to what scientists do.

10. What new questions could you investigate?

Investigation 5:

The Special Properties of Water

Key Question
Before you begin, first think about this key question.

Why is water special?

Materials Needed

For this investigation the materials your group will need are listed for each station.

Think about your previous experiences with water. What unique properties does it have? How do other materials interact with water? How does water change when it is heated or cooled? How do its special properties make life possible?

Write your thoughts in your journal. Share and discuss your thoughts with your group and with the rest of your class. Make a class list of your ideas.

Investigate

1. Each group will investigate a special property of water at each station.

Here are the questions you will be investigating:

Station A: What happens when water interacts with other common substances?

Station B: What happens when objects are placed in water?

Station C: What happens when water is cooled?

Station D: What kind of particle is a water molecule?

Station E: How is frozen water different from liquid water?

Station F: What kind of particle is a water molecule? (Part 2)

Station A

1. You will add a small quantity of each of the following items to water, one at a time:

   - vegetable oil
   - food coloring
   - dry fruit drink mix
   - sand

   Before you add the material to the water, write a prediction of what you think will happen.

   a) Record your prediction in your journal. Give the reasons for your prediction.

   Observe the water after each addition.

   Stir the water and observe again.

   Observe how the substances interact with the water.

   b) What items dissolved in water?

   c) What items did not dissolve?

   d) How did stirring affect each trial?

Inquiry

Hypotheses

When you make a prediction and give your reasons for that prediction, you are forming a hypothesis. A hypothesis is a statement of the expected outcome of an experiment or observation, along with an explanation of why this will happen. A hypothesis is not a guess. It is based on what you, as the "scientist," already know.

Materials Needed

- four 500 mL beakers or similar containers
- vegetable oil
- food coloring
- dry fruit drink mix
- sand
- stirrers
- source of hot water
- ice

Wear goggles.
Do not eat or drink any materials used in investigations. Hot water should not be scalding hot. Dispose of all materials properly.

2. Repeat Step 1 using ice water and hot water. Be sure to make a prediction. If you think that the temperature of water will affect what happens, explain why.

a) Record your predictions and reasons in your journal.

b) How did hot water affect the ability of each substance to dissolve?

c) How did cold water affect the ability of each substance to dissolve?

d) What properties of water does this station demonstrate?

Station B

1. You will add a quantity of each of the following items to water, one at a time:

- granite chips
- pumice
- leaf
- dry soil
- plastic item

Before you add the material to the water, predict what you think will happen and why.

a) Record your prediction in your journal. Give the reasons for your prediction.

b) After you have added each item, record your observations.

c) What did you find surprising about your results?

d) What properties or characteristics of water does this station demonstrate?

Station C

1. Fill a soda can halfway with water and a second soda can halfway with sand. The sand and water should be at room temperature.

Use a thermometer to measure the temperature of the water and the sand.

a) Record the initial temperatures.

2. Place each soda can and thermometer in a 1000-mL beaker of ice water.

Materials Needed

- granite chips
- pumice
- leaf
- dry soil
- plastic item
- five 500 mL beakers or similar containers

Clean up spills immediately.

Materials Needed

- two soda cans
- two thermometers
- two 1000-mL beakers
- sand
- container of ice
- timing device
- graph paper

3. Observe the temperature every minute for 25 minutes. Add ice to the ice water as needed

   a) Record your observations.

   b) Graph your results. Plot time along the horizontal axis (*x* axis) and temperature on the vertical axis (*y* axis).

   c) Describe the two graphs. Which substance cools faster, sand or water?

   d) What properties or characteristics of water does this station demonstrate?

Station D

1. Inflate a balloon and rub it against your hair or a sweater. You have put an electric charge on the balloon.

2. Put the "charged" balloon near a thin stream of running water.

   a) What do you notice about the interaction between the balloon and the water?

   b) How do you explain this?

   c) What properties or characteristics of water does this station demonstrate?

Materials Needed
- balloon
- water faucet

Station E

1. Put some water in a container.

   Put a piece of ice in the water and observe what happens.

   a) Compare and contrast ice with liquid water.

2. Measure the mass of a graduated cylinder or measuring cup.

   Pour 100 mL of water into the cylinder.

   Measure the mass of the cylinder and the water sample.

   Calculate the mass of the water.

   Calculate the density of the water in grams per milliliter by dividing the mass by the volume.

   a) Record your observations and your calculations.

3. Fill a graduated cylinder two-thirds full with very cold water.

   Note the volume in your notebook.

   Measure the mass of a block of ice.

Materials Needed
- container of water
- ice cube
- 100 mL graduated cylinder or measuring cup
- 100 mL water
- balance scale
- block of ice

Wipe up spills immediately.

Inquiry

**Quantitative and
Qualitative Observations**

*Observations dealing with
numbers are called quantitative
observations. An example of a
quantitative observation is mass,
measured in grams, and volume,
measured in milliliters.
Qualitative observations refer to
the qualities of the object.
Observing whether an object
floats or sinks in water is a
qualitative observation. Some
observations can be made either
quantitatively or qualitatively. In
this investigation you are making
both quantitative and qualitative
observations.*

Materials Needed

- sewing needle
- container of tap water
- capillary tube
- container of colored
  water

Handle the needle with care.
Wipe up spills.

Without spilling or splashing the water, tilt the graduated
cylinder and slide the ice block into the water. Hold the ice
just below the surface of the water with a toothpick or
pencil point. Note the new volume of the water.

a) Subtract the volume of water from the volume of
"ice plus water" to obtain the volume of the ice block.

b) Calculate the density of the ice in grams per cubic
centimeter by dividing the mass of ice by the volume
(1 cc of water = 1 mL of water).

4. Use your observations in Steps 1 to 3 to answer the
following questions:

a) How does the density of ice compare to the density of
water? (Note that 1 mL is equivalent to 1 cm^3.)

b) How does the difference between the density of ice and
water explain your observations in Step 1?

Station F

1. Try floating a
needle on the
surface of a
container of tap
water.

a) How did you
place the needle
on the water
surface to get
the needle to
float?

b) How do you
explain this
property of water?

2. Place a capillary tube
in a solution of
colored water.

a) Record your
observations.

b) Explain your
observations.

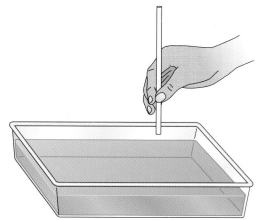

Summary

1. Revisit your answer to the key question of this investigation.

   a) Add any new information that you now have as a result of the activities you have completed. Summarize your findings in the form of a table.

2. Present your findings to the class.

Digging **Deeper**

THE PROPERTIES OF WATER

You probably take water for granted because it is so common, but water is a very unusual substance. Its most spectacular property is that ice floats in water. You probably think that's no big deal, but water is almost the only substance in the universe for which the solid floats in the liquid!

→

As You Read...
Think about:

1. How does the heat capacity of water compare with the heat capacity of rock?
2. How effective is water as a solvent?
3. Why is the water molecule called a polar molecule?
4. Why is the density of ice less than the density of water?
5. What special property of water allows certain insects to walk on water?

Water is also very unusual in several other ways. For example, the heat capacity of water is higher than just about any other substance. The heat capacity of a substance is the amount of heat you need to add to a mass of material to raise its temperature by a given amount. The heat capacity of water is more than twice the heat capacity of natural mineral and rock material. This tends to even out temperature differences on Earth, from day to night and from summer to winter. Water is also the best all-around solvent. More solid substances dissolve in water than in any other liquid.

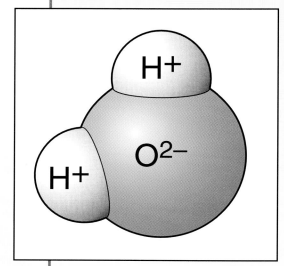

Molecule of water.

Water consists of molecules with the composition H_2O (two small atoms of hydrogen and one larger atom of oxygen). The two hydrogen atoms are bonded very strongly to the oxygen atom. The three atoms are not arranged in a straight line; instead, they form an angle, as shown in the diagram. The electrons that orbit around the three atoms are more strongly attracted to the oxygen atom than to the hydrogen atoms. Electrons have a negative electric charge. This gives the oxygen "side" of the water molecule a slightly negative electric charge. The hydrogen "side" of the water molecule has a slightly positive electric charge. Molecules like this, with one side positive and the other side negative, are called polar molecules. This is why the stream of water was affected by the electric charge on the balloon in Station D of this investigation.

In nature, electric charges of the same sign repel, and electric charges of different signs attract. When water molecules bond together in a regular structure to form solid ice, the positive sides of the molecules are attracted to the negative sides of adjacent molecules. The bond that is formed is called a hydrogen bond. It is weaker than the bonds between the hydrogen and the oxygen but still strong enough to cause water to freeze into ice.

Why does ice melt when the melting temperature is reached? In nature, every atom or molecule undergoes a vibration, or "jiggling," because it has thermal energy. The strength of the vibration increases with temperature. When the temperature is high enough, the ice melts, because the thermal vibration of the molecules becomes so strong that the hydrogen bonds are broken. In the ice structure, the molecules have a relatively open arrangement. When the ice melts, the molecules become free to pack together more closely. That is why water is denser than ice.

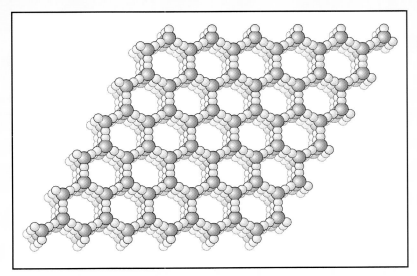

The atomic structure of ice.

The water molecules in liquid water attract each other. Inside the liquid, any particular water molecule is acted on by attractive forces from all directions. It is different for a molecule right at the water surface, however. It is attracted by molecules below it and beside it, but not from above. This makes the surface tend to shrink parallel to itself. This shrinkage force is called surface tension. Have you ever watched a soap bubble being made by waving a bubble wand? It is stretched out at first, but as soon as it leaves the wand, it becomes a sphere. That is because surface tension is making the whole bubble pull inward on itself. You were able to float the needle in the water because, as the needle started to sink downward, the surface tension pulled it upward, almost as if the water surface had been a thin sheet of rubber.

The rise of water you observe in a thin tube is called capillary action, or capillarity. It is another effect of surface tension. If you looked closely, you noticed that the surface of water in the tube curves upward around its edge. (This curved surface is called the meniscus.) To understand capillarity, you need to know that there is more to surface tension than just at the water surface. There is also surface tension in the film of water that is in contact with the glass of the tube, and also in the film of air that is in contact with the glass of the tube. The surface tension of the air film is stronger than the surface tension of the water film. That causes the meniscus to be pulled upward along the glass surface, and water rises up in the tube. Capillarity explains why a piece of cloth or a paper towel gets wet when you hang its lower edge in water. The tiny passageways between the fibers act as capillary tubes! When the material is treated with a water repellent the surface tension between the air and the material is reduced. Then water is no longer drawn up into the fibers.

Review and Reflect

Review

1. Explain what happens when oil is spilled on water.

2. Name at least three substances that dissolve in water.

3. What special properties of water did you investigate that provide evidence that water is a polar molecule?

Reflect

4. Water is a good solvent. How does this fact relate to water pollution?

5. You live on the shore of a large lake. Would you expect the temperature of the air near your home to be cooler or warmer than inland during the winter months? During the summer months? Explain your answer.

6. Why would the fact that ice is less dense than water be important for the survival of freshwater fish and other organisms that live in cold climates?

7. Use what you learned about water in this investigation to convince someone that water is a very valuable resource.

Thinking about the Earth System

8. How do the properties of water influence its role in the Earth system?

Thinking about Scientific Inquiry

9. Use examples from this investigation to explain the difference between qualitative and quantitative observations.

10. Describe two pieces of evidence that you have that water is a special substance.

Investigation 6:

The Quality of Your Water Resources

 Key Question
Before you begin, first think about this key question.

How healthy is your local watershed?

As you found in the last investigation, water is a good solvent. Many materials readily dissolve in it and are carried along as the water flows from the source to its destination. Professionals who monitor your water supply test the water for impurities at key points along the way. Where could your water supply pick up impurities? What impurities do you think you might find in your water supply?

Share your thinking with others in your group and with your class.

Materials Needed

For this investigation your group will need:

• water samples

• water-testing kits and tools

 Investigate

1. Before you begin this investigation, you need to revisit what you did when you mapped the watershed for your area in Investigation 3.

Determine exactly:

- what feeds into your local watershed,
- what is the condition of your watershed, and
- whom you can contact with any questions.

2. Water analysis is performed at various stages of the water distribution system to ensure that the quality of water is safe. The analysis might include tests for:

- dissolved oxygen
- turbidity (clarity)
- pH (acidity or alkalinity)

- hardness
- chemicals
- bacteria.

As a group, decide which tests you could perform in the classroom.

a) In your journal record the test that you plan to perform, the reason that you chose the test that you did, and the exact testing procedure. Have it checked by your teacher for safety and accuracy and make any changes necessary.

3. Use your local watershed map to determine where you should take and test water samples.

Remember that you are trying to find out what your local water quality is like at key points in the watershed.

a) Write down your sampling plan, and why you made your decisions. Have it checked for safety and feasibility. Make any necessary changes to your plan.

4. You will need to acquire a collection of the water samples.

Your class might go on a field trip to key areas, or someone may be able to collect the samples (with the accompaniment of an adult) for the entire class.

5. When your samples arrive in class, conduct your tests.

a) Record the information for each part of the watershed that you are testing. You might find it particularly useful to record your data directly onto a map of your local watershed.

Do not proceed with any test until the teacher has approved it. If using test kits or equipment, follow all instructions carefully. Wash hands when finished.

Inquiry

Consider Evidence

In this investigation you are asked to answer questions about water quality in your community. You have gathered some evidence that can help you answer these questions. However, the evidence you have may not answer all the questions. Looking for patterns and relationships within the evidence may lead to new questions to investigate.

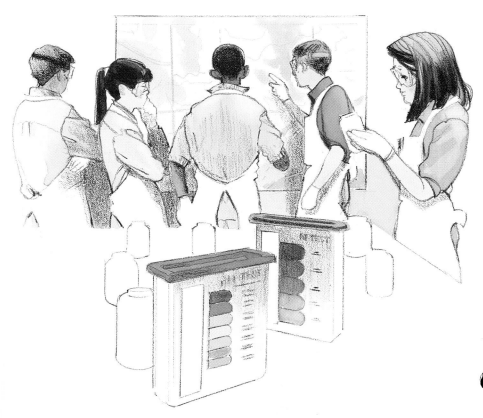

6. Review what you have found out about the water quality in different parts of your watershed.

   Answer the following questions. Provide the evidence that you have.

   a) How does the water change as it proceeds downstream?

   b) How would you describe the quality of your water as it heads toward you?

   c) What do you think needs to be done in your area to ensure a regular supply of clean fresh water?

   d) What do you think are the water quality issues in your area? What is your evidence for that?

   e) What other questions still need to be asked?

7. An important piece in identifying a water supply issue in your area is public knowledge and perception of that issue.

   Ask a selection of adults in your community if they know of any water supply issues in your area.

   a) Record the responses to this informal survey for later use.

WATER QUALITY
What Is "Good" Water?

The term "water quality" is used to describe how good a water source is for human use. The idea of water quality would be easy to deal with if all water sources were either "good" or "not good." The real world is more complicated than that. There are all degrees of "goodness" of water. That is because many substances can affect water quality, and their concentrations can range from very low to very high. The quality of water required also depends on its intended use. For example, the quality of water that is meant for drinking ("potable" water) is different from the quality of water that can be used for the irrigation of fields.

Pollutants

Some of the substances that affect water quality are called pollutants. Pollutants are mostly substances that get into water by human activities. The number of toxic chemicals that are produced and used by humans is enormous. Many of these toxic chemicals are used in ways that cause them to be added to surface water or groundwater.

Cleaning up sources of pollution takes enormous sums of money. Contaminated soil or sediment has to be removed. Sometimes it is just put in special places that are sealed off from the environment forever (we hope!). Sometimes the toxic substances are converted into nontoxic substances by chemical processes.

Have you ever thought about what happens to the salt that is put on roads in winter in the northern areas of the United States? It is dissolved by later rainfall. Some of it enters

As You Read...
Think about:
1. *Why is it difficult to decide if water is "good" or "bad"?*
2. *What is meant by "potable" water?*
3. *What are possible sources of chemicals in water? Name at least two sources.*
4. *What are possible sources of harmful bacteria in water?*

rivers and is carried to the ocean, and some of it is added to groundwater. Pollution by road salt is a major problem in some watersheds.

Harmful Microorganisms

Microorganisms that cause illnesses also affect water quality. Bacteria are single-celled animals that cannot be seen with the human eye except through a microscope. Some kinds of bacteria are the most dangerous microorganisms. They usually get into water supplies when untreated sewage mixes with the water supply. It is not only a matter of human wastes from leaky sewer pipes. Dog and cat droppings are also deposited on land inside and outside the city.

Natural Solutes

Naturally occurring substances also affect water quality. Even raindrops are not pure water. As they fall they pick up tiny dust particles and also harmful substances like acid that are in the atmosphere. Gases in the atmosphere (carbon dioxide, sulfur dioxide) can also dissolve in raindrops to form acid rain. When the rainwater comes in contact with soil and rock material, some of that material dissolves in the water. Substances that are dissolved in water are called solutes. The concentration of natural solutes depends mainly on two factors: the composition of the soil and rock material, and how long the water is in contact with that material. Calcium makes water "hard," although not harmful. Hard water has a noticeable taste, and it can leave deposits inside pipes and tanks. The softest and purest water comes from areas that are far from where humans live, and have rock like granite or quartz sandstone that does not dissolve easily in water.

Review and Reflect

Review

1. What did your tests reveal about the local water?

2. What surprised you the most about what substances entered your water-supply system?

3. Where do polluting chemicals come from in a water-supply system? Name a source in your community, and one in a community different from yours.

Reflect

4. Why is it important to know what chemicals are in water?

5. How did the quality of water change as it headed toward your community?

6. What are the water-quality issues in your area? What is your evidence for that?

Thinking about the Earth System

7. On your *Earth System Connection* sheet, write any new connections you found between water as a resource and Earth systems.

Thinking about Scientific Inquiry

8. Give an example of how you used each of the following inquiry processes in the investigation:

    a) forming a question,

    b) making a prediction,

    c) collecting evidence.

Investigation 7:

Cleaning up Water Resources

Key Question

Before you begin, first think about this key question.

How is your water supply cleaned and tested?

In the previous investigation you discovered that impurities of many kinds can enter the water system. What can be done to remove these impurities before the water reaches your home? What is done with the water after you have used it?

Materials Needed

For this investigation your group will need:

- water filtering materials
- containers for water
- water-test kit

Investigate

1. Check the telephone book to find out what agencies in your area are responsible for cleaning up the water supply. You need to look for the water purification plant, and the wastewater treatment facility.

   If possible, contact these agencies and ask for a person from the facility to visit your classroom.

An alternative would be to take a field trip to your local water or wastewater treatment plant.

2. You will need to prepare questions for your visitor before he or she comes to visit (or before you go on a field trip to the plant). Remember to focus on the local water-quality issues that you have discovered from your own research.

Think about these points as you generate your list of questions for your visitor:

- Where is water cleaned?

- How is water cleaned?

- Who makes sure that the water is clean?

- What assurance do you have that your water supply is clean?

- What particular issues of water quality or supply are important in your area?

a) List your questions in your journal and save them for later.

3. Before your visitor comes to your class, it is also important for you to have experience with the process of cleaning up a sample of "contaminated" water.

Each group will be provided with a sample of simulated wastewater. There will not be anything in the water that is harmful, but the water will not look or smell like water that anyone would want to drink!

4. Before you get started with purifying your water sample, you need to get a good sense of what is in it. Use your senses (except for taste!) in a safe and careful way to find out what might be in your sample.

a) Record your results.

5. Once you have used your senses to get a good idea of what might be in your water sample, take a good look at the water purification materials on the supply table.

Discuss the following points with your team and record your answers in your journal:

a) Which tools might be useful for getting particular contaminants out of the water sample?

Follow the teacher's instructions for how to smell the sample safely.

b) What type of device could you set up that would allow the water to come in contact with the water-cleaning materials?

c) What types of devices already exist for cleaning up water? How do these work?

d) How will you know that the contaminants are no longer there?

e) What will you do with the waste materials?

Inquiry

Designing and Conducting an Investigation

Scientists must think very carefully about the design of their investigations to make sure that the results are reliable. Often, they repeat a test several times to ensure reliable results. When designing a system for cleaning and testing water it would be very critical to have consistent and accurate results.

6. Design and make your system for cleaning and testing water. Be sure that you can defend your method of cleaning the water sample to others.

a) Record your cleaning and testing system in your journal. Have your teacher check it for safety and workability. Make any modifications necessary.

7. With the approval of your teacher, clean up the water sample using the system you designed.

   Decide how you will collect evidence that your cleaning system removes specific contaminants from the water.

   a) Record your observations in your journal.

8. When you have cleaned up your water sample as well as you can, prepare a display showing what the problems were with your sample, how you cleaned up the water, and the evidence that you collected for demonstrating that the water is clean.

   Be prepared to present your display when you have your visitor from the local water-cleaning facility in the class or to the rest of the class.

Do not proceed with any plan for cleansing the water until the teacher has approved it. Do not drink water samples, even if they appear to be clean. Clean up spills. Wash hands when finished.

Digging Deeper

TREATMENT OF DRINKING WATER AND WASTEWATER

Most people in the United States get their water from municipal (city and town) water systems. Most people in rural areas, and also some in suburbs, get their water from their own wells, which tap shallow or deep groundwater.

The water that is supplied from municipal water systems comes mainly from three sources: streams and rivers; natural lakes or artificial reservoirs; and groundwater, pumped from large wells. Lakes and reservoirs that are located in unpopulated areas far from cities and towns usually have the highest-quality water. That is also true for streams and small rivers in unpopulated areas. Large rivers usually have lower-quality water, because of pollution from upstream areas. Ground water is contained in underground materials called aquifers. The quality of ground water varies a lot from place to place, depending on the quality of the surface water that supplies the aquifers.

As You Read...
Think about:
1. What are the sources for water that supply municipalities?
2. How can fine sediment be removed to increase the quality of drinking water?
3. What substances in water make it "hard"?
4. How is household wastewater treated?

Treatment of Drinking Water

Some sources of drinking water are of such high quality that not much treatment is needed. Usually, an addition of small amounts of chlorine are sufficient to kill any harmful bacteria or other microorganisms. Other water sources, especially large rivers, have higher levels of pollution. Such sources require more to bring the water up to the needed level of quality. River water usually contains fine sediment particles in suspension. The water can be passed through filtration materials, like sand, to remove the fine sediment. Filtering the water also tends to remove bacteria. Another way of removing the fine sediment is to let the water sit in large basins while the sediment slowly settles to the bottom. Sometimes this settling process is speeded up by adding certain chemicals that cause the fine sediment particles to clump together into larger particles. The larger particles settle faster than the original fine particles.

One problem in any system for water treatment is the difficulty of removing dissolved salts. All natural waters contain some dissolved substances, like sodium, calcium, magnesium, and iron. When the concentrations are too high, however, the water may taste salty. Calcium and magnesium make the water "hard," which makes washing with soap or detergents more difficult. Salt can be removed from water by various processes in what are called desalination plants. Drinking water produced by desalination is considerably more expensive than natural fresh water. It is used mainly in developed countries, like the United States, Israel, and Saudi Arabia, where fresh water is scarce but the ocean is nearby. Some coastal cities in California are beginning to use desalination for part of their water supply.

Wastewater Treatment

Most of the water that is used in homes and businesses is put into either municipal sewers or home septic

systems. Most of that water is polluted to some extent, because it comes from clothes washing, bathing, and toilets. In earlier times, sewage was put directly into the ground, into rivers, or into the ocean, without any treatment. As populations have grown, however, the need for wastewater treatment has increased as well.

Home septic systems consist of a large underground tank, where anaerobic bacteria (those that do not need oxygen) gradually break down most of the solids. The remaining liquid waste flows out into what is called a leach field, where the water flows out from porous underground pipes into the ground. This water still contains pollutants and harmful microorganisms. Some of these are removed as the water flows through soil and rock, but in many places they reach groundwater supplies and add to problems of water pollution.

Municipal sewage is treated in special wastewater treatment plants. There are several common methods of treatment. Also, the level of treatment varies greatly.

- In primary treatment, all that is done is to put the water in large tanks or ponds to let the solid material, called sludge, either float to the surface or settle to the bottom. The water is then usually chlorinated, and the sludge is treated and disposed of in various ways.

- Most wastewater undergoes secondary treatment as well. The most common method is to sprinkle or trickle the water over a bed of sand or gravel. As the water filters downward, it is put into contact with oxygen and microorganisms, which work together to break down the organic matter in the water.

- In a few places, the water undergoes tertiary treatment, which involves a variety of processes to purify the water even further. After tertiary treatment, the water can be pure enough to drink!

1. Streams, rivers, lakes, and artificial reservoirs are sources of municipal water.

2. Screens are used to remove debris.

3. Settling removes fine sediment. Chemicals are added to speed the process.

4. Filtration also removes fine sediment.

5. Chlorine is added to kill microorganisms.

6. Water is pumped through water mains.

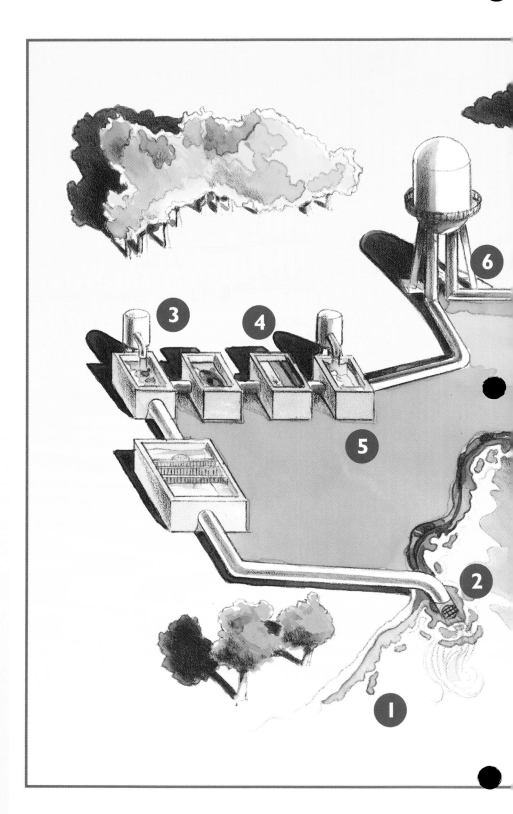

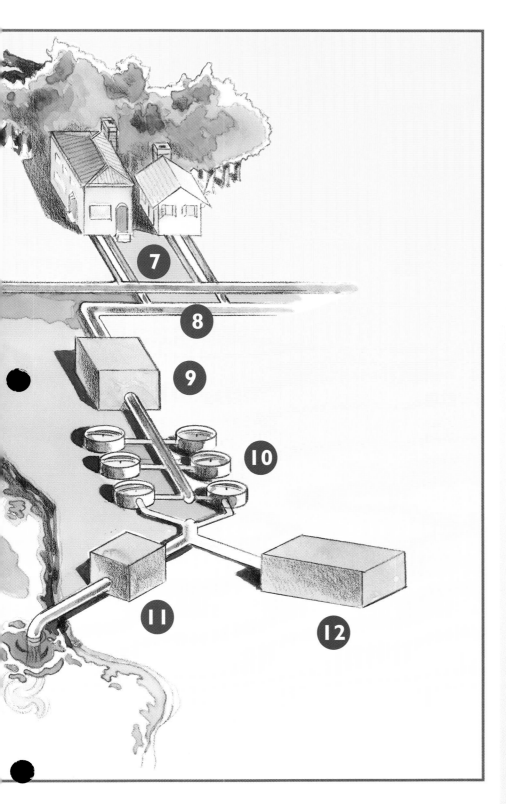

7 Clean drinking water is delivered to homes.

8 Pipes carry wastewater away.

9 Primary treatment takes place in large tanks. Solid materials settle as sludge.

10 During secondary treatment air and bacteria break down sewage.

11 Water is returned to the lake or river.

12 Tertiary treatment uses chemicals, filters, and radiation to purify water even further. It can be pure enough to drink.

Review and Reflect

Review

1. Look again at the key question: How is your water supply cleaned and tested? Write down what you have learned from your investigation that provides answers.

2. What kinds of things do water treatment facilities test for?

3. What kinds of problems can certain pollutants cause if they get into the water supply?

Reflect

4. Do you think that residential groups (everyday citizens) should become involved in water management issues? Why? How can they get involved?

5. How can a developed country such as the United States help others in developing countries that might not have a consistently clean water supply?

Thinking about the Earth System

6. How do you think a change in the Earth's water system (hydrosphere) affects other systems (atmosphere, geosphere, and biosphere)?

7. How do the atmosphere, geosphere, and biosphere affect the hydrosphere?

Thinking about Scientific Inquiry

8. Why is a carefully designed and reliable test for water quality important?

9. Where in this investigation did you:

a) Use tools?

b) Show evidence and reasons to others?

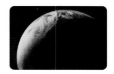

Investigation 8:

Water Conservation Partnership Plan

Key Question

Before you begin, first think about this key question.

How can you maintain your water resource?

You have investigated and read about water. What can you do in your community to maintain it as a resource?

Materials Needed

For this investigation your group will decide what materials are needed.

Investigate

1. At this point in the module, you should have a good understanding of the following key ideas:

   • where fresh water comes from;

   • what the properties of water are that make it such a valuable substance;

- where fresh water can be found on the planet;
- what a watershed is, and what your local watershed is like;
- what contaminants can get into the water supply;
- how contaminants in the water supply can be detected;
- some of the natural and commercial methods of cleaning a water supply;
- why water quality is important, and to whom it is important.

Review the work that you have produced over the course of the module, as well as all of the entries in your journal to check your knowledge of these points.

a) In your journal record any additional information you need to answer the above questions.

2. In this final investigation, you are going to pull together all of your knowledge about water and your experiences with the water supply in your area to develop a water quality partnership plan for your community.

Because there are so many different issues related to water quality, you may decide that it would be more beneficial if each group in your class specialized in just one part of the plan.

You can then put everyone's work together at the end to have a complete plan for the community.

3. To begin your work on your plan, you need to return to your water-issues survey from your previous investigation (Investigation 6, Step 7). As a class, list what you found to be key water-supply issues in your area.

Review these issues, and decide in which part of the plan each group will specialize.

a) List the name of the responsible group after its issue.

Before you begin any work on your plan, you may need to get help on ways in which you can develop it.

One useful way could be to make a flowchart of the issue and all key points which have an impact on the issue.

Here is one example:

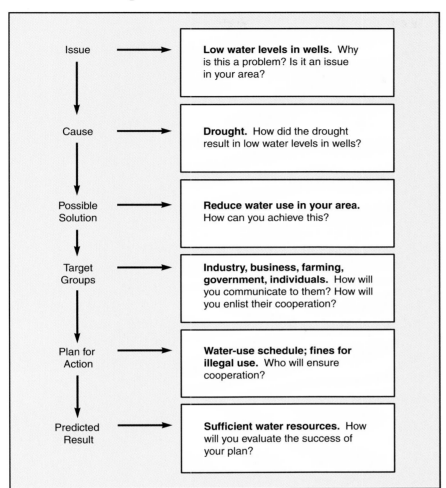

4. As you can see from the sample flowchart, your role as students must be a realistic one. You can come up with a well-thought-out plan and present it to those in authority over the water supply in your area. However there is only so much that you as an individual can do to carry out the plan.

It is important that you have realistic expectations of what you can and cannot do with regard to maintaining your local water supply before you begin your plan.

5. Once you have agreed on which group is doing what issue, focus on making a flowchart (or other outline) of your plan.

You have a number of resources already collected, but you may find that you need to do more research as you

develop your plan. For example, you may find, through searching on the Internet, that another community in another part of the world has the same water issue as your community.

Be sure to consult for advice as you need it.

a) What did that community do to resolve the issue?

b) What guidance can you get from the way they solved their water problem?

6. As you think about and develop your plan, you will also need to be thinking about what goes into the final version. Here are items that you will need to include:

- your water supply issue;
- why this is a local water supply issue (your research on the Internet);
- water test results;
- local news items;
- interviews with water authority officials;
- survey information from the community (water quality standards for your area, etc.);
- past work on this or similar issues in other geographic areas;
- how members of the community can help to resolve the issue;
- your specific role to help resolve the issue;
- timeline for the plan;
- who will implement and enforce the plan;
- what your plan will accomplish (impact on the water supply);
- who will receive your plan;
- approximately how much money you think it will take to get your plan started. (How could you find out?)

With your colleagues, discuss all these points, and form a plan that will include them. Consult your teacher if you need advice.

a) Record your plan in your journal.

7. When you have finished your plan, you need to present it to your classmates and, ideally, the person or persons for whom the plan is intended (local government official, water treatment operators, or community members). You may also want to share your findings with a wider audience (the whole school, parents, and the community).

You need to prepare your presentation in such a way that all the items included in your plan are clear and easily understood. You might choose to do this in a variety of ways.

8. After you have done what you can about your water quality plan (and this may take quite a long time), think back on the science that you needed to know to identify your issues, make your plan convincing, carry it out, and evaluate its success. For example:

a) How did you know what fed into your watershed?

b) How did you know what the water quality was in your area?

c) How did you figure out possible substances that could have gotten into any local groundwater?

d) What could account for any drought-related or flood-related issues?

e) What properties of water could explain why water quality and quantity are such important and controversial issues?

Review and Reflect

Review

1. According to the plans proposed by all of the groups, who were the important target groups for maintaining water as a resource?

2. What are important water issues in your community?

Reflect

3. Is your water plan realistic? Explain your answer.

Thinking about the Earth System

4. What effects would your water quality plan have on the biosphere? Atmosphere? Hydrosphere? Geosphere?

Thinking about Scientific Inquiry

5. How would you continue the inquiry process in this investigation?

Reflecting

Back to the Beginning

You have been investigating water as a resource in many ways. How have your ideas about water as a resource changed from when you started? Look at the following questions and write down your ideas now:

• How is water used?
• Where is water found?
• How is water part of the Earth system?
• How is a supply of safe, usable water ensured?

Thinking about the Earth System

At the end of each investigation, you thought about how your findings connected with the Earth system. Consider what you have learned about the Earth system. Refer to the *Earth System Connection* sheet that you have been building up throughout this module.

• What connections between water as a resource and the Earth system have you been able to find?

Thinking about Scientific Inquiry

You have used inquiry processes throughout the module. Review the investigations you have done and the inquiry processes you have used.

• What scientific inquiry processes did you use?
• How did scientific inquiry processes help you learn about water as a resource?

A New Beginning

Not so much an ending as a new beginning!

This investigation into water as a resource is now completed. However, this is not the end of the story. You will see water where you live, and everywhere you travel. Be alert for opportunities to observe water as a resource and add to your knowledge and understanding.

The Big Picture

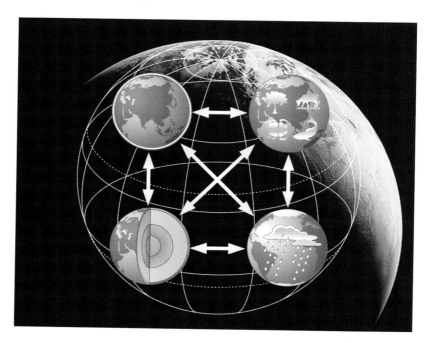

Key Concepts

Earth is a set of closely linked systems.

Earth's processes are powered by two sources: the Sun, and Earth's own inner heat.

The geology of Earth is dynamic, and has evolved over 4.5 billion years.

The geological evolution of Earth has left a record of its history that geoscientists interpret.

We depend upon Earth's resources—both mined and grown.

Glossary

Acid rain – Rain that has a pH of less than 4.

Anaerobic bacteria – Bacteria that can live without oxygen.

Aqueduct – A system of large surface pipes and channels used to transport water.

Aquifer – Any body of sediment or rock that has sufficient size and sufficiently high porosity and permeability to provide an adequate supply of water from wells.

Atmosphere – The layer of gas that surrounds the Earth. The atmosphere is a mixture of several gases.

Atom – A unit of matter composed of a nucleus and orbiting electrons; the smallest indivisible form of an element that maintains that element's chemical characteristics.

Bacteria – One-celled microorganisms that do not have a formal organization of their nuclear material.

Biosphere – The part of the Earth System that includes all living organisms (animals and plants) and also dead and decaying plant matter.

Capillarity – The rise of water in a thin tube. Also called capillary action.

Chemicals – Elements or compounds. The smallest part of an element that retains its characteristics is an atom. The smallest part of a compound that retains its characteristics is a molecule.

Chlorine – A substance used to kill harmful microorganisms in water.

Condensation – The process of changing from a gas to a liquid.

Conserve – To save.

Design – A plan for investigation. This could be a laboratory experiment, model, simulation, field study, or other type of investigation.

Dissolve – To put a solid into solution.

Distillation – The removal of impurities from liquids by boiling.

Drainage basin (also watershed) – The land area from which rainfall collects to reach a given point along some particular river.

Drainage divide – An imaginary line on the land surface that separates one drainage basin from another.

Earth System – A term used to describe the Earth as a set of closely interacting systems, including all subsystems, like the geosphere, lithosphere, atmosphere, hydrosphere, and biosphere.

Evaporation – The process of changing from a liquid to a gas.

Evidence – Data that support or contradict a scientific hypothesis or conclusion.

Fair test – A fair test (a test that is objective and systematic) is an experiment in which only one variable is tested at a time. A fair test also involves a control, a well-defined research question, collection and verification of data, and repeated trials.

Geosphere – The part of the Earth System that includes the crust, mantle, and inner and outer core.

Glacier – A large and long-lasting mass of ice that is formed on land by compaction and recrystallization of snow, which flows downhill or outward under the force of its own weight.

Gravity – The gravitational force of attraction of the Earth for a mass or body of material at or near the Earth's surface.

Ground water – Water contained in pore spaces in sediments and rocks beneath the Earth's surface.

Hard water – Water that has a high concentration of calcium and magnesium ions.

Heat capacity – The amount of heat you need to add to a mass of material to raise its temperature by a given amount.

Hydrogen bond – A weak chemical bond between a hydrogen atom in one polar molecule and an electronegative atom in a second polar molecule.

Hydrosphere – The part of the Earth system that includes all the planet's water, including oceans, lakes, rivers, ground water, ice, and water vapor.

Hypothesis – A statement that can be proved or disproved by experimental or observational evidence.

Inquiry – The process of finding answers to questions through a variety of methods. These can include research, observations, fair testing, using models, asking experts, or many other methods.

Inquiry processes – The methods used by scientists to find answers to questions. They include hypothesizing, observing, recording, analyzing, concluding, communicating, and others.

Inquiry questions – Questions designed to be answered through a Systematic, scientific process.

Ion – An atom that has an electric charge.

Meniscus – The curved shape of the top surface of a liquid in a narrow container.

Mineral – A naturally occurring solid material that consists of atoms and/or molecules that are arranged in a regular pattern.

Model – A representation of a process, system, or object that is too big, too small, too unwieldy, or too unsafe to test directly.

Modeling – The process by which a representation of a process, System, or object is used to investigate a scientific question.

Observations – Data collected using the senses.

Ocean – Huge bodies of salt water that cover about three-quarters of the surface of the Earth.

Permeability – A measure of the ease with which a fluid can be forced to flow through a porous material.

Pesticide – A chemical that kills insects.

pH – A number between 0 and 14 that indicates how acidic a solution is. The lower the number the more acidic a solution is.

Polar molecule – A molecule with a negative charge on one side and a positive charge on the other.

Porosity – A measure of the percentage of pores (open spaces) in a material.

Precipitation – Water that falls to the Earth's surface from the atmosphere as liquid or solid material in the form of rain, snow, hail, or sleet.

Prediction – A reasonable estimate of the outcome of a scientific test. Predictions are based upon prior knowledge, previous experimental results, and other research.

Qualitative properties – Features that are described without using numbers, such as color, odor, and so on.

Quantitative properties – Features that are described by making measurements using numbers, such as mass (number of grams), length (number of meters), and so on.

Raw sewage – Untreated sewage.

Record – To make a note of observations and events. Recording can be done on paper, electronically or through other means of communication such as video, sound recording, or photography.

Sludge – The solid waste material that is separated from water in the treatment of wastewater.

Solute – The substance dissolved in a solution.

Solvent – A substance, usually liquid, that can dissolve another substance.

Surface tension – The property of liquids in which the exposed surface tends to contract or shrink to the smallest possible area.

Surface water – Liquid fresh water that resides temporarily on the Earth's surface in the form of rivers and lakes.

Topographic map – A map showing the natural and man-made configuration of a land surface, other features of the land surface, commonly by use of contour lines, colors, and symbols.

Transpiration – The emission of water vapor from pores of plants as part of their life processes.

Wastewater – Water after it has been used.

Wastewater treatment – A series of physical, biological, and chemical processes used to remove impurities from wastewater.

Water – A pure substance consisting of molecules of two hydrogen atoms bonded to one atom of oxygen.

Water cycle – The cycle or network of pathways taken by water in all three of its forms (solid, liquid, and vapor) among the various places where is it temporarily stored on, below, and above the Earth's surface. Also called hydrologic cycle.

Watershed – A drainage basin. The direction in which water drains from land.

Water treatment – Physical and chemical methods of removing impurities from the drinking water supply.

The American Geological Institute and Investigating Earth Systems

Imagine more than 500,000 Earth scientists worldwide sharing a common voice, and you've just imagined the mission of the American Geological Institute. Our mission is to raise public awareness of the Earth sciences and the role that they play in mankind's use of natural resources, mitigation of natural hazards, and stewardship of the environment. For more than 50 years, AGI has served the scientists and teachers of its Member Societies and hundreds of associated colleges, universities, and corporations by producing Earth science educational materials, *Geotimes*–a geoscience news magazine, GeoRef–a reference database, and government affairs and public awareness programs.

So many important decisions made every day that affect our lives depend upon an understanding of how our Earth works. That's why AGI created *Investigating Earth Systems*. In your *Investigating Earth Systems* classroom, you'll discover the wonder and importance of Earth science. As you investigate minerals, soil, or oceans — do field work in nearby beaches, parks, or streams, explore how fossils form, understand where your energy resources come from, or find out how to forecast weather — you'll gain a better understanding of Earth science and its importance in your life.

We would like to thank the National Science Foundation and the AGI Foundation Members that have been supportive in bringing Earth science to students. The Chevron Corporation provided the initial leadership grant, with additional contributions from the following AGI Foundation Members: Anadarko Petroleum Corp., Baker Hughes Foundation, Barrett Resources Corp., BPAmoco Foundation, Burlington Resources Foundation, Conoco Inc., Consolidated Natural Gas Foundation, Diamond Offshore Co., EEX Corp., ExxonMobil Foundation, Global Marine Drilling Co., Halliburton Foundation, Inc., Kerr McGee Foundation, Maxus Energy Corp., Noble Drilling Corp., Occidental Petroleum Charitable Foundation, Parker Drilling Co., Phillips Petroleum Co., Santa Fe Snyder Corp., Schlumberger Foundation, Shell Oil Company Foundation, Southwestern Energy Co., Texaco, Inc., Texas Crude Energy, Inc., Unocal Corp. USX Foundation (Marathon Oil Co.).

We at AGI wish you success in your exploration of the Earth System!

Michael J. Smith
Director of Education, AGI

Marcus E. Milling
Executive Director, AGI